## Hide and Seek

# Find the
# Polar Animal

By Cate Foley

Children's Press
A Division of Grolier Publishing
New York / London / Hong Kong / Sydney
Danbury, Connecticut

Photo Credits: Cover pp. 5, 6, 7, 13, 14, 15 17, 18, 19, 21 © Animals Animals;
pp. 9, 10, 11, 21 © Index Stock
Contributing Editor: Jennifer Ceaser
Book Design: Nelson Sa

Visit Children's Press on the Internet at:
http://publishing.grolier.com

Library of Congress Cataloging-in-Publication Data

Foley, Cate.
    Find the polar animal / by Cate Foley.
      p. cm. — (Hide and seek)
    Includes bibliographical references and index.
    Summary: Challenges the reader to examine photographs and find the polar animals hiding in their
      surroundings, including seals, foxes, and penguins.
    ISBN 0-516-23093-X (lib. bdg.) — ISBN 0-516-23018-2 (pbk.)
    1. Zoology—Polar regions—Juvenile literature. 2. Camouflage (Biology)—Juvenile
literature. [1. Zoology—Polar regions. 2. Camouflage (Biology) 3. Picture puzzles.] I.
Title.

QL104.F66 2000
591'.0911—dc21
                                                                        00-024581

# Contents

1 Resting on the Rocks      4

2 An Animal with White Fur      10

3 Animals on the Shore      12

4 Sleeping in the Snow      16

5 New Words      22

6 To Find Out More      23

7 Index      24

8 About the Author      24

Look closely.

Do you see the animal resting on the rocks?

4

5

This seal swims in **icy** seas.

It also lies in the warm sun.

The seal hides by blending in with the rocks.

Apollo School Library
10100 Des
Des Plains
(847)

7

Look closely.

Can you find the animal sitting in the snow?

This fox has **thick**, white fur.

The fur helps the fox to hide in the snow.

It also keeps the fox warm.

Look closely.

Do you see a group of animals on the **shore**?

12

13

Penguins stay safe on the shore.

The feathers on their backs are dark like the rocks.

15

Look closely.

Can you spot the animal sleeping in the snow?

17

This polar bear makes its bed in a **snowdrift**.

The hill of snow **protects** the bear from the cold wind.

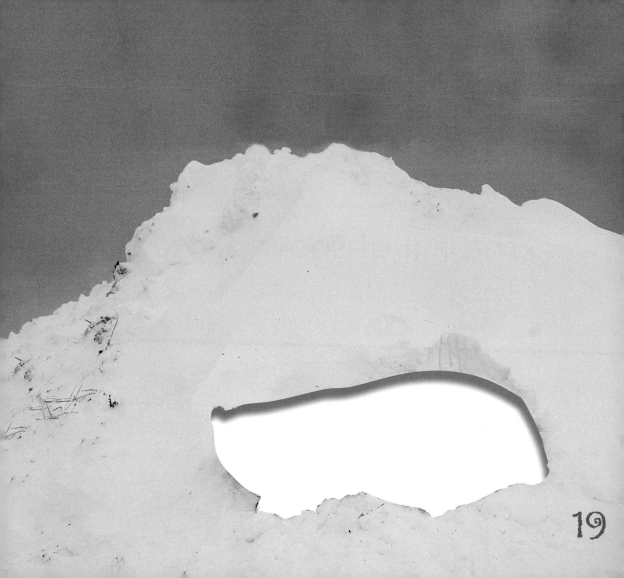

19

What if you visited the North or South Pole?

Which **polar** animal would you like to see?

20

21

# New Words

**icy** (**eye**-see) something that is covered
with ice

**polar** (**poh**-ler) having to do with the
North or South Pole

**protects** (pro-**texts**) keeps safe

**shore** (**shor**) a place where the ocean
meets the land

**snowdrift** (**snoh**-drift) a hill of snow
made by the wind

**thick** (**thik**) full and warm

# To Find Out More

**Books**
*How to Hide a Polar Bear & Other Mammals*
by Ruth Heller
The Putnam Publishing Group

*The Arctic* (Look Who Lives In)
by Alan Baker
Peter Bedrick Books

**Web Sites**
**Arctic Wildlife Portfolio**
http://www.mnh.si.edu/arctic/html/wildlife.html
Learn about your favorite polar animals. This site has pictures, facts, and games.

**Wild Arctic Activities**
http://www.seaworld.org/arctic/index.html
This site contains lots of information and activities about polar animals.

# Index

feathers, 14
fox, 10
fur, 10

icy, 6

penguins, 14
polar, 20
polar bear, 18
protects, 18

seal, 6
shore, 12, 14
snowdrift, 18

thick, 10

**About the Author**
Cate Foley writes and edits books for children. She lives in New Jersey with her husband and son.

**Reading Consultants**

Kris Flynn, Coordinator, Small School District Literacy, The San Diego County Office of Education

Shelly Forys, Certified Reading Recovery Specialist, W.J. Zahnow Elementary School, Waterloo, IL

Peggy McNamara, Professor, Bank Street College of Education, Reading and Literacy Program